TO

_____

FROM

_____

DATE

_____

A Sportsman's Call

Steve Chapman

PAINTINGS BY THE
HAUTMAN BROTHERS

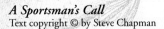

A Sportsman's Call
Text copyright © by Steve Chapman

Artwork copyright © by The Hautman Brothers, courtesy of MHS Licensing, and may not be reproduced without permission.

Published by Harvest House Publishers
Eugene, Oregon 97402
www.harvesthousepublishers.com

ISBN 978-0-7369-6216-2

Design and production by Koechel Peterson & Associates, Inc., Minneapolis, MN

Portions of this text are excerpted from *A Hunter's Call* (Harvest House Publishers, 2005), *Fish Tales* (Harvest House Publishers, 2007), and *Pursuing the Prize* (Harvest House Publishers, 2007), all by Steve Chapman.

Printed in China

14 15 16 17 18 19 20 21 / FC / 10 9 8 7 6 5 4 3 2 1

CONTENTS

Of Flies and Men

HUMANS AND FROGS have at least two things in common: fun and flies. We say, "Time flies when you're having fun." They say, "Time's fun when you're having flies!" Thankfully, they have been chosen to consume the disgusting insects. For us, unless we are yawning on a fast-moving motorcycle, we are privileged to find joy in using flies. We humans who fish can feed the appetites of our adventurer hearts by throwing out fake flies with lines and leaders and rods.

More than half the intense enjoyment of fly-fishing is derived from the beautiful surroundings, the satisfaction felt from being in the open air, the new lease of life secured thereby, and the many, many pleasant recollections of all one has seen, heard, and done.

CHARLES F. ORVIS

There's something very satisfying and restful about gently and accurately laying a chosen bait on the surface of a slow-moving pool. That alone is plenty of reward. Add the sudden explosion of water and the exciting pull of the line, and you have the necessary ingredients to make the icing that goes on the adrenaline cake.

Stepping down off a bank into the cold, uneven bed of a trout stream and feeling the weight of the water press my rubber waders against my legs is a step of bliss for me. And how often it is needed! Getting away from the phone, fax machines, the Internet, and the busy streets filled with exhaust fumes creates a precious time. Sometimes a fellow just needs it. Occasionally a person has to put the brakes on and take a breather before he or she breaks! If not, a mind can snap like 10-pound test line being yanked by a 90-pound striped bass!

All fishermen will appreciate Psalm 23:2-3. The passage was custom written for them:

> *"Some go to church and think about fishing, others go fishing and think about God."*
>
> TONY BLAKE

"He makes me lie down in green pastures [taking a break from fishing and having lunch]; He leads me beside quiet waters [Yes! Back to fishing]. He restores my soul [Caught one!]."

Why is this psalm so important? Here's one reason: Unlike frogs, who know how to sit motionless for long periods of time in order to outsmart a skittish insect, most humans do not naturally embrace the skill of resting. We so easily yield to the temptation of being overactive. The balance between work and rest has been sadly lost.

It is important to take note that a primary word in the definition of "restores" is "rest." We can take a valuable lesson from our little green friends. We would do well to be content, at least every once in a while, with ceasing from our labors. Everyone needs the benefits of taking a break by having fun. May you see the fun in stopping for a while to have…that is…to cast some flies.

My Pa he ist fished an' fished!
An' my Ma she said she wished
Me an' her was home; an' Pa
Said he wished so worse'n Ma.

Pa said ef you talk, er say
Anything, er sneeze, er play,
Hain't no fish, alive er dead,
Ever go' to bit! he said.

Purt' nigh dark in town when we
Got back home; an' Ma says she,
Now she'll have a fish fer shore!
An' she buyed one at the store.

Nen at supper, Pa he won't
Eat no fish, an' says he don't
Like 'em.—An' he pounded me
When I choked!...Ma, didn't he?

JAMES WHITCOMB RILEY
from *The Fishing Party*

*I now believe that fishing
is far more important
than the fish.*
ARNOLD GINGRICH

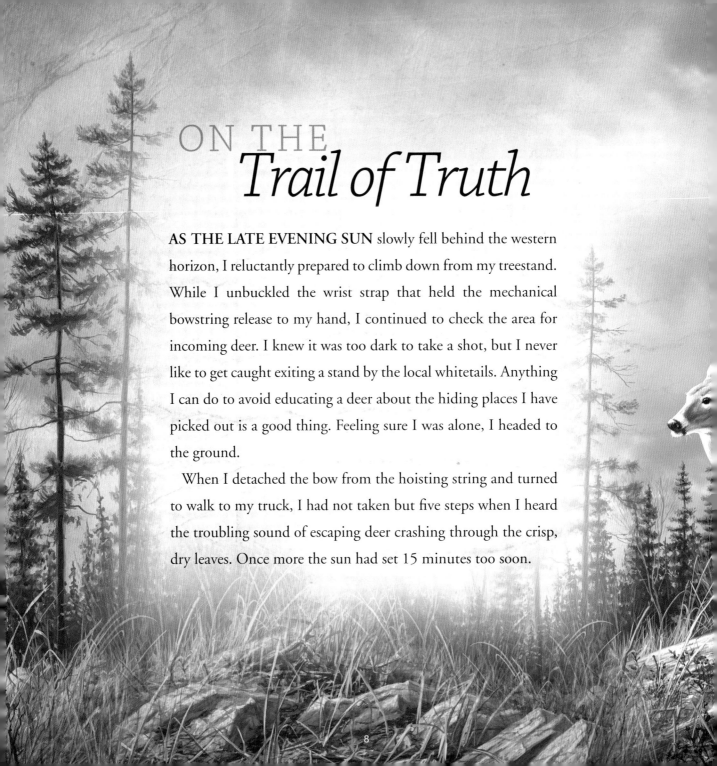

ON THE
Trail of Truth

AS THE LATE EVENING SUN slowly fell behind the western horizon, I reluctantly prepared to climb down from my treestand. While I unbuckled the wrist strap that held the mechanical bowstring release to my hand, I continued to check the area for incoming deer. I knew it was too dark to take a shot, but I never like to get caught exiting a stand by the local whitetails. Anything I can do to avoid educating a deer about the hiding places I have picked out is a good thing. Feeling sure I was alone, I headed to the ground.

When I detached the bow from the hoisting string and turned to walk to my truck, I had not taken but five steps when I heard the troubling sound of escaping deer crashing through the crisp, dry leaves. Once more the sun had set 15 minutes too soon.

Because my timing was off…again…it was another disappointing evening of deer hunting. It wasn't a super letdown, though, because I had a great time trying. But I did feel downhearted because so many days of the season had passed, and my tag was yet to be punched. There were deer in the area, but they weren't showing up while I still had shooting light.

I finally shared my dilemma with a more experienced bow hunter. I mentioned him in my first book, *A Look at Life from a Deer Stand*. His name is Mark Smith. His advice was short on words but long on insight.

"You're not going deep enough in the woods, good buddy," Mark said with his Louisiana drawl. "You probably like the edge of the field 'cause it's easier, plus you probably like it 'cause the light hangs on a little longer."

> *The woods were made*
> *for the hunter*
> *of dreams,*
> *the brooks*
> *for the fishes of song.*
>
> SAM WALTER FOSS

"Well, you're right about the light thing," I said and then countered with, "but I can't say that I set up near the field edges 'cause it's easy. I do it 'cause the deer like to come to the fields in the evening to browse. They're always arriving late though."

Mark smiled. When I finished my whining he said, "That's just my point. The deer you're hunting are smart critters. They'll hang back in the woods until it's dark enough for them to feel safe to go out into the open. This is especially true for the bigger, more mature bucks. If you want to get an arrow into one of the whitetails on that farm, you're gonna have to take your climber farther back into the woods and catch them earlier in their trip to the soybeans."

What Mark said made so much sense that I nearly hugged him. But because I don't like getting beat up, I kept my arms to myself. I just thanked him profusely.

An evening or two later I headed back to the farm. I relocated my portable climber about 75 yards farther back into the timber. About 15 minutes before the woods turned too dark to legally shoot, which is much sooner than at the field edge in the early part of the season, a trio of sizable deer casually strolled under my stand. They had exited their bedding area among the clutter of cut, fallen treetops and were slowly heading toward the soybeans. Just as the light went out inside the woods, I found the doe I arrowed lying a mere 40 yards from the tree where I had placed my climber.

I have thought of Mark's words from time to time when I sense my world becoming narrow, when I get so caught up in the day-to-day grind that I forget what's important. Then I know it's time to go deeper—to commune with God, to connect with my loved ones, and to take the time to appreciate life.

There is a poignancy, a tinge of sadness
*   intermingled with the exhilaration of a successful hunt,*
*   that has the aura of sacredness.*
Confronting these feelings, the paradoxical counterpoise
*   of life and death, loss in the midst of capture,*
*   is fundamental to how and why I am a hunter.*

MARY ZEISS STANGE

DEER HUNTERS RARELY SIT on a deer stand thoughtless and brain dead. We "wrap ourselves around the hunt" by constantly watching the woods, carefully looking for the slightest movement. We mentally rehearse our shooting methods, and we take note of weather and wind. Our minds are busy. This active approach creates pure excitement from the first moment of a hunt to the last.

While there are some unquestionably wonderful by-products of keeping a vigil on a deer stand, such as learning how and why to redeem the time, seeing deer is the ultimate reason I gladly linger there. The anticipation of sighting the subtle movement of brownish-colored fur amid the thicket or catching the flicker of a white-tipped tail in the distance—pure heaven. And it's this unique aspect of deer hunting that has taught me more about how to enjoy the rest of life than nearly anything else.

Catching Trouble

I ONLY WANTED TO SEE if I could pester the slithery intruder as it wiggled its way past my boat. The snake was about 30 yards off my starboard side and, from my aft perch, I could see it was probably about four feet long. The open-face reel neatly and quietly unraveled the line as my bait flew over the snake and dived into the water. It had landed just inches beyond the critter. When the line settled on the lake it fell right onto the snake's back. It slowed as I began to gently reel in.

I'm not quite sure how I managed to do it but the treble hook on my lure snagged the target and the next thing I knew my rod tip bent sharply down and I had myself a situation. The catch and release method of fishing sure started looking like a good idea. However, try as I would, I could not separate my unwanted guest from my hook.

I decided to reel him in closer to the boat and try using my oar to knock him off the expensive lure which was too valuable to lose. When it was within a few feet of my hull I lifted the slimy thing out of the water and held it out at rod's length. He writhed wildly in protest.

Thinking I might be able to sling the thing off, I decided to attempt a cast. It would save me from having to dig for the oar. As I brought the rod and reel over the boat to get into a casting position, the inevitable happened. The snake fell off my hook and right into the middle of the boat!

Needless to say, I headed for the highest point of my rig, the swivel seat behind me. I had no idea what kind of snake I had inadvertently invited on board, but I knew things were getting serious.

As the bewildered creature searched for cover, I went for the oar. Beating it to death was not my preference, but I was more than willing to have a change of heart. Then I remembered my hook. I thought, Why not resnag him and try lifting him out of the boat?

At this point I was very open to forfeiting my lure and feeling safe again.

So that's what I did. With hopes of not snagging the carpet, I placed the lure over the snake's back and gave it a jerk. Yes! It was hooked. With that accomplished I lifted him out of the boat, dropped him into the water, and quickly cut the line. Somewhere today there is a snake slithering around the lake with a colorful ornament permanently stuck in its side. I hope its friends are impressed!

I learned a big lesson that day. Toying with a serpent is not a wise thing to do. Next time I see one invading my space, I'll just watch it from afar.

Miss Watson she took me in the closet and prayed,
but nothing come of it. She told me to pray every day,
and whatever I asked for I would get it. But it warn't so.
I tried it. Once I got a fish-line, but no hooks.
It warn't any good to me without hooks.

Huck Finn in *The Adventures of Huckleberry Finn*
by Mark Twain

May the holes in your net
be no larger than the fish in it.
IRISH BLESSING

Mayonnaise Baked Fish with Tropical Salsa

GEORGIA VAROZZA

Slather both sides of fish with mayonnaise and salt and pepper to taste.
(Roasted garlic mayonnaise is especially good if you can find it.)
Wrap fish loosely in a tinfoil tent and place package on a cookie sheet.
Bake fish in 375 degree oven until done.
Fish will flake easily when cooked. Do not overcook.

Tropical Salsa

2 papayas, peeled, seeded, and diced small
1/2 green bell pepper, diced small
1/2 red bell pepper, diced small
1/2 red onion, diced small
1 jalapeno pepper, seeded and diced small
1/2 cup fresh cilantro, chopped
juice from one orange
juice from 1 to 2 limes
1 tablespoon cumin
2 teaspoons kosher salt
1 teaspoon black pepper

Mix all ingredients. Keeps in the refrigerator for several days. Serve over baked fish.

ALL IN THE WRIST

One of my favorite parts of the fishing routine is casting. There is something in my psyche that allows me to feel very satisfied when I see my bait splash a mere inch or two from where I wanted it to fall. To know my eye/hand coordination is working well is most rewarding. If all I got done at the lake was a good day of accurate casting, I could go home with no reason to complain. Hooking a fish, of course, takes the joy to the next level, but I refuse to complain if it doesn't happen.

Luck affects everything.
Let your hook always be cast;
    in the stream where you least expect it
    there will be a fish.
              Ovid

They took their way towards the house
on the opposite side of the river,
in the nearest direction;
but their progress was slow, for Mr. Gardiner,
though seldom able to indulge the taste,
was very fond of fishing,
and was so much engaged in watching the
occasional appearance of some trout in the water,
and talking to the man about them,
that he advanced but little.

Jane Austen, *Pride and Prejudice*

> *"Everything that lives and moves will be food for you.*
> *Just as I gave you the green plants, I now give you everything"* (GENESIS 9:3)...
> *Hunting, therefore, is something that has been part*
> *of human life since the very beginning, and God gave it*
> *to us so that we could benefit from it and enjoy it.*
>
> JIM GRASSI

It Takes One to Hunt One!

THE WILD TURKEY was Benjamin Franklin's choice for the bird that would be recognized as one of our national symbols. Why he chose it as a nominee or why it never received that place of honor would be interesting to know. I'm sure one could dive into the archives and find out, but why do that when it's a lot more fun to guess?

Starting with the reasons for rejection, I can think of only two possibilities. One, it's just not the prettiest bird on the planet. With a face like that on our dollar bills and presidential emblems, it would be tough to look at them for very long and find patriotism welling up inside. The poor thing was not graced with handsomeness. The male, especially, got a serious whack in the kisser with the ugly stick. And to the die-hard lovers of the wild turkey, I'm sorry but that thing—that wattle—hanging off an old gobbler's face is really gross. I think they make medicine for that! I will admit though, from the neck down, it's a beautiful creature, which could be said of a lot of humans.

Second, the flight of a wild turkey does not match that of the final choice, the Bald Eagle. There's something about the high-flying ability of the eagle that stirs in us a desire to rise above things such as ignorance and poverty. It moves us deep in our hearts. On occasion the broad-breasted turkey must take to the air to escape danger, but they don't sail very far. Though pretty in flight as they leave the roost at daylight and whoosh overhead on their way to their kitchen table, they just can't get to the heights that an eagle can. Of course, if the eagle was packing enough food on its breast to feed a family of five, it too would have a hard time flapping its way into the stratosphere. The wings are there, the wind is waiting, but the "pot breast" of a turkey gets in the way.

For whatever reason, you won't find the heavy, homely, and horrifically ugly face of a turkey on your silver dollar. Nor will it ever grace the banners that wave over this nation. The two birds in question have a lot to offer but the bottom line is that *flying* was chosen *over* food. And that's fine with me.

Don and Eddy talked me into going along... warning me that I would never be the same after the attempt— and they were right!

Regarding the possible reasons that Ben Franklin presented the turkey as a good representative of America's positive traits, there are a few that seem logical. Could it be that the turkey was initially considered because it was a plentiful food source for the people who lived here and for those who eventually settled on this continent? In my experience as a turkey hunter, there is a consistency about the breast meat that is both tender and tasty.

For people who fashioned their own arrows, turkey feathers for fletching were the best. The length and strength of its quill and the width of the plume added to the arrow's durability and accuracy of flight. Furthermore, arrow-making was more than the construction of a practical tool for hunting and self-defense. It was also a work of art. Turkey feathers were often used as vanes on the shaft because they held ample color and eyecatching marks. This was true then and remains so today.

Of all the reasons the wild turkey should have gotten the votes needed to occupy the office of "top bird," I can't help but wonder if Mr.

Franklin's main reason for putting the *Meleagris gallopava* on the ballot was rooted in his love for hunting it. I have a feeling that after many frustrating attempts to harvest a turkey, he developed a level of respect for the bird that was similar to the amount of esteem others gave to him as a leading citizen of the nation. It seems reasonable to believe he had had some exciting encounters with the incredibly effective eyesight of a turkey. And it's conceivable that he had discovered how nearly impossible it is to see a bird that stays on the ground through the daytime, feeding beneath the underbrush well below eye level of the average-sized man. As far as I'm concerned, if Franklin's feelings about the turkey were grounded in his sincere regard for its elusiveness, that alone is good enough for me. I say it's not too late to call for another vote!

I admit there was a time when I didn't put turkey and deer hunting on the same line in terms of the excitement level involved. The reason was simple…I had never tried it. Then one day my friends Don Scurlock and Eddy Richey talked me into going along for a hunt during spring season in Tennessee. They warned me that I would never be the same after the attempt—and they were right!

That first hunt was unforgettable. Don and Eddy instructed me that two things were extremely important. One, camo cover for every part of the body was absolutely necessary. Don even covered his eyes. And, following his example, I shrouded my pump shotgun with camo tape. Without the proper concealment, there was no way to blend in with the surroundings and fool a turkey's highly sensitive peepers.

Second, they told me that when the bird is coming in, the slightest movement would likely spook it and send it scampering. The blink of an eye or a trigger finger sliding around to push the shotgun safety button had the potential to ruin the opportunity. I was cautioned that once a gobbler fixed on a hen call and decided to approach, my shooting position had to be already established, otherwise I would blow it.

There was enough exciting emotion in just the instructions Don and Eddy gave to cause my heart some considerable palpitations. I ventured on with them to the fields that morning on my first turkey hunt. As we walked on the dirt road well before daylight, we kept our talking to a whisper. Don had "put the birds to bed," meaning he watched them from a distance the evening before and knew where they had flown to roost. Knowing they were in the trees on a bluff nearby, we took care not to disturb their slumber.

In the darkness, Eddy put two decoys out in the field, and then the three of us took our places along the tree line. Just after first light, Don began using a gift he possessed that is nothing less than remarkable. He had studied and practiced the wild turkey's language so well that he, with his man-made devices, could speak to them as if he were one of their own. With a light, dainty clucking sound, Don broke the morning silence. His "waking up" call initially got no response. But he knew what he was doing. He waited a minute or two and with the flat, waterproof mouth call made of tape and latex rubber, he spoke again. Behind us, a bird responded. I froze. Eddy was motionless. Don slowly looked over at me and though I couldn't see his face behind the mesh camo mask, I could tell he was smiling. It was the way he held his head that told me his heart was racing faster than the pistons in a screaming Indy car.

Suddenly, I heard my very first sound of the swish of turkey wings in flight as a bird sailed off the bluff and glided down into the field. The grace of its soaring was impressive. So was its size. I didn't realize how tall a wild turkey stood. I wouldn't have noticed had I not been crouched low against a big oak. From where I was sitting, the eyes of the hen that had landed in the meadow appeared to be looking down at me. It was an awesome sight.

I was already in the shooting posture and had been there since we sat down. I took the instruction about minimizing my movement very seriously and was trying to be a good student. The problem that arose was excruciating, however. After about 20 minutes in one position, my body started to protest. My derriere had lost its feeling and the numbness was creeping up my back and was on its way to my brain. But to move would have spelled disaster. Although my arms wanted desperately to shake, I forced myself to hold steady and hoped relief would come quickly.

Finally, a bearded bird descended into the field. The male is the only legal game allowed during the spring season, and the sight of one was welcome. As he landed near the hens, they briefly scattered. It was as if they were well aware that he came around only when he wanted "something." Except for this special time in a gobbler's life, when "love" is all they are after, they usually stay away from the females and travel in bachelor groups.

Finding himself around several attractive hens, the male began his ritualistic strutting. With his tail at full fan, his head changed colors from pale gray to a brilliant red, along with some white and a hue of blue. It was a sight to behold. The problem for the three of us sitting there waiting to send him to turkey heaven was that he was too far away. Don was careful not to talk too much with his calls for fear of saying the wrong thing and causing the gobbler to run off. All we could do was sit by and hope he meandered over within range.

Suddenly things started falling into place. They were working their way around the field to where we sat. By then, the mixture of painful numbness and explosive excitement had started doing weird things to my entire body. Knowing I couldn't move, I wanted to shake like I had grabbed hold of a live electric wire. I was loving this new experience! In the stream of pure adrenaline that was rushing through my brain, I saw a reflection of the future. I could see all the seasons of springtimes yet to come, and I knew where I wanted to be when they arrived. I wanted to be at the edges of fields, tucked away in my camouflage among the leaves and branches, doing what I was doing at that very instant. Before I had ever pulled the trigger on one of these birds, I had become a bona fide, no-holds-barred turkey hunter. I had been "spurred."

…that old bird might be ugly, but he's smart!

As it turned out that morning, none of us were able to score. When the gobbler got within 50 yards, he saw something he didn't like and scampered off to another part of the farm in search of companionship. Sadly, the three of us gathered our decoys, seat pads, and wounded egos and headed home. But it was still exciting, and I have been on many successful turkey shoots since then. Every time it's a thrill.

Some final observations about the wily old gobbler…I have to admit I have a lot in common with him. For one thing, that old bird might be ugly (did I just insult myself?), but he's smart! And there's another thing that impresses me about him. It's in his nature to run at the very first sign of danger, and I have never seen him ignore that attitude. A mature male turkey is just that because he doesn't stay around for one extra second if he thinks his life or safety is in jeopardy. I've arrowed a lot of deer because they stood there a moment too long after detecting trouble. I got the best of

their curiosity. Not so for a woods-wise gobbler. He's gone at the first hint of trouble. I deeply admire the gobbler's attitude of willingness to forego the next grub worm, juicy bug, or even a fleeting, extra glance at the source of danger. He knows it's the key to his survival. I want to be like him. May I never forget that quickly running is the best way to steer clear of temptation.

With that worthy goal in mind, I will consider it a great compliment the next time spring season arrives in Tennessee and my sweet wife, Annie, looks at me in my boyish getup of head-to-toe camo and facetiously says, as she often does, "Turkey—it takes one to hunt one!"

Little Dog, Little Boy

STEVE CHAPMAN

Little dog, little boy
Billy Wayne called him Watchman Roy
Close as ice cream in a cone
Where Billy went Roy went along

Strong right arm
Broken stick
Billy threw it far
Roy brought it back
A simple game they both enjoyed
Little dog, little boy

And in the night when Billy dreamed
He had no fear of evil things
'Cause at his side was Watchman Roy
Little dog, little boy

Mama was mad 'cause Roy's paws
Left red clay mud on her kitchen walls
She grabbed a broom,
  tried to beat him like a drum
Billy laughs, Roy runs

Tall grass fields and a thousand trails
Spend a winter day chasing cottontails
When evening came
  he loved to tell his huntin' stories
Happy dog, tired boy

And in the night when Billy dreamed
He had no fear of evil things
'Cause at his side was Watchman Roy
Little dog, little boy

Now these are the tales my Grandma told
'Bout Grandpa Billy, her heart and soul
But today he went to find Ol' Roy
She said, "A little dog needs a little boy."

Now in the night when Billy dreams
He'll have no fear of evil things
'Cause at his side is Watchman Roy
Little dog, little boy

My dear old dog, most constant of all friends.

WILLIAM CROSWELL DOANE

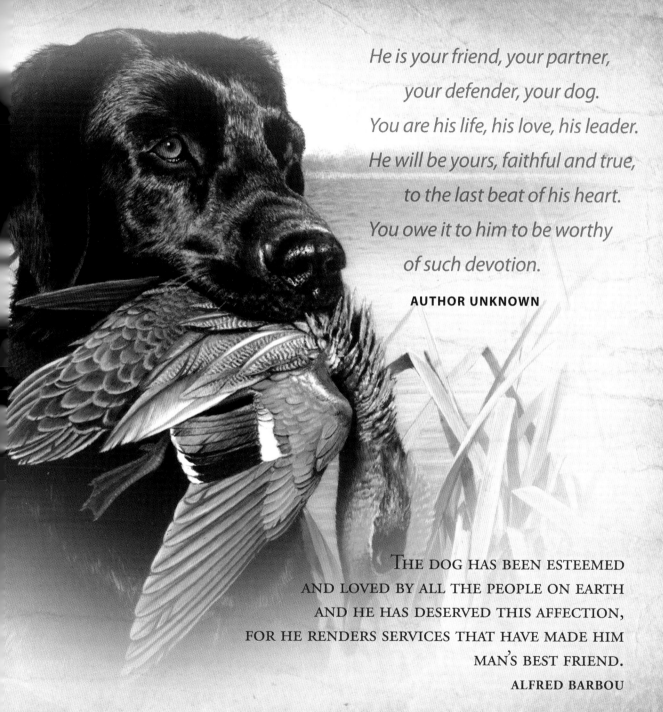

He is your friend, your partner,
your defender, your dog.
You are his life, his love, his leader.
He will be yours, faithful and true,
to the last beat of his heart.
You owe it to him to be worthy
of such devotion.

AUTHOR UNKNOWN

THE DOG HAS BEEN ESTEEMED
AND LOVED BY ALL THE PEOPLE ON EARTH
AND HE HAS DESERVED THIS AFFECTION,
FOR HE RENDERS SERVICES THAT HAVE MADE HIM
MAN'S BEST FRIEND.

ALFRED BARBOU

29

BASIC
Training

UNTIL I MOVED to Tennessee in 1974, my fishing had been limited to throwing a line from the banks of farm ponds and the shores of the Ohio River. I also had some brief experiences with standing in a trout stream and tying myself into knots. Never had I ventured onto the water in a boat.

In the Nashville area there are two nice lakes. Old Hickory and Percy Priest are a wonderful pair of opportunities for those who enjoy big lake fishing. When I was told that the coves where an angler could find solitude and success were nearly innumerable, I longed to drop a line into them. However, I didn't own a vessel or know anyone who did, so I could only dream about getting out there…until I heard about the rentals at Elm Hill Marina. The idea rolled around in my head for weeks. The one thing that kept me from going straightaway to the marina was not the money. It was the fact that I didn't have a clue how to operate a motorized boat.

Maybe it was the extra strong coffee that day, but one morning I decided to drive out to Percy Priest and make my dreams come true. I went into the office, plopped down my money, signed the papers, and followed the agent down to the dock. Within minutes the motor was puttering in neutral—the agent had started the engine to make sure it was operating well enough for a day's workout. I didn't have a clue how to fire it up.

The fellow stepped out of the boat and said, "Turn the handle counterclockwise to go forward and clockwise to reverse. See you at four this afternoon." With a wave, I climbed in and sat down in front of the engine. I had at least seen enough pictures to know where I was supposed to sit. Other than that, I was at a loss.

My hands shook as I rolled the throttle into reverse. Well…I thought I was putting it into reverse. I had overlooked the fact that when facing forward, one has to think backward to work their hands behind them. "Bang!" Up against the dock I plowed. Quickly I rolled the handle the other way, and I shot across the water like a surface torpedo. I was heading straight for a huge, beautiful sailboat. I jerked the handle sideways and barely missed the hull of the tall boat. Then I heard a scream.

Somehow I had ended up going nearly at full throttle—in reverse—right at a brand-new ski boat. The lady aboard was frantic and her voice screeched, "No! Get away!" Thankfully, I reversed the roll of the throttle, and by the grace of heaven I just missed certain disaster and a probable lawsuit. I ended up back by the dock.

The agent must have heard the commotion because he appeared in a flash. As he approached the dock, he realized he'd rented his boat to a complete novice (a nice way of saying "idiot"). I'll never forget how exasperated he sounded when he threw his cigarette into the water and said, "O.K., step one!" With the skill of a seasoned mariner, in just a few brief moments of instructions on the basics, he had me on my way to the coves I had dreamed about. Though it started with the ingredients for a nightmare, the day turned out quite nice.

To expect to go from an unenlisted sailor straight to the captain's chair is a stunt no swabbie would ever try. How grateful I was for the rental agent's willingness to teach me the basics, and even more grateful that he trusted me to continue on my adventure.

Fishing on the River was not a tame experience. The water was deep. It rushed over huge boulders the size of trucks. It swirled and foamed. If a person fell into it, surviving would be iffy. Consequently, when I was a little shaver, the River terrified me; Dad would move from rock to rock like a mountain goat; but I watched well-back on the bank and prayed fervently that he wouldn't fall into the River. Sometimes I wept out of fear that he would. As I came to respect the danger of the River, but also to enjoy its beauty and be thankful for the trout dinners it furnished, I learned to move from rock to rock like Dad did. Nevertheless, I gave that roaring River its space and didn't tempt it; I never quit watching Dad and other fishing companions to make sure they hadn't slipped and fallen into the River.

HAP LYDA
from Lyda Lore: *A Heritage of Hunting & Fishing, Volume II*

Paul & Andy's Cosmic Marinade and Dressing

BETTY FLETCHER

It doesn't get any easier or more delicious.

Spread a thin layer of mayonnaise and a thin layer of mustard on the surface of the salmon fillet. Add a pinch of sea salt. Bake, skin side down, at 400 degrees for 15 to 20 minutes per inch of thickness.

This marinade/dressing has many uses. Try it with fish, green salads, and pasta dishes.

1/4 cup balsamic vinegar
1/8 cup (2 tablespoons) water
5/8 cup (10 tablespoons) olive oil
1 teaspoon salt
1 to 2 teaspoons Dijon mustard
2 to 6 cloves of garlic, crushed (to taste)

Place all ingredients in shakable container and agitate. (The proportions match those of a Good Seasons dressing bottle. This is a simple way to mix and dispense the marinade.)

Options for use with salmon

Use as marinade for baked salmon. Allow to marinate for at least 2 hours before baking.

Use as a dressing for salmon while barbecuing. Apply liberally during cooking.

Add cooked salmon and steamed vegetables to your favorite pasta and add the marinade to taste for a great pasta salad meal.

Fishing provides that connection with the whole living world. It gives you the opportunity of being totally immersed, turning back into yourself in a good way. A form of meditation, some form of communion with levels of yourself that are deeper than the ordinary self.

TED HUGHES

My Old Hunting Hat

Someone once said, "I don't believe in luck…but I do believe in my old huntin' shirt!" Now I don't embrace the idea of depending on a charm, but I do have a severely tattered hat that I have worn for years. For some strange reason I feel better when I'm hunting under it. It's ugly and floppy and the camo pattern has nearly faded to the color of raw cotton. Still, I choose its cover above all other lids I own.

I suppose the real reason I prefer my old hat is simply because we have been many miles together, and it has served me well. It has absorbed my sweat during long stalks for deer, shaded my eyes against the brilliant rising sun while scanning the horizon for incoming mallards, and offered a warming shield against bitter cold winds that accompany winter days in pheasant fields.

Someday I'll be forced to retire my aging fedora. When that time comes, I will not toss it into a trash bin. Instead, with permission from my wife, it will find its resting place in our hallway curio where other valuable treasures are stored—a place of honor for a true friend.

I pray that my life will be meaningful to people just like my old hat has been to me. Comfortable, warming, protecting, absorbing, available, and enduring. And when my time is finished, I would be honored to be stored away in their hearts where they keep fond memories.

First-Time
CALLER

THE OLD LOGGING ROAD on the 400-acre farm I was hunting ran straight along a ridgeline for quite a distance and then made a wide, sweeping turn through the woods. On one side of the road was a steep slope that dropped off the ridge down to a water source. I placed my climbing stand on the opposite side, about 60 yards off the road in the open timber because very often I would watch deer come up out of the ravine and get onto the logging road that was lined with huge white oak trees. Usually they would feed along the 100 yards or so where the acorns had dropped onto the road, and then they'd make a right turn into the woods and walk through the area where I was set up. They favored that route because it led them downhill into a bottom where a heavy thicket provided plenty of cover for them to bed down for the day.

When ten o'clock in the morning arrived, I had not seen a sign of fur. I was about to start my dismount from the tree when movement caught my eye to the left. Suddenly I saw one lone, antlered deer step onto the logging road and casually begin enjoying a midmorning feast of freshly fallen acorns. Thankful that I had no particular deadlines to meet, and that I could stay put for the excitement, I slowly stood to my feet and prepared for a possible close-up encounter with what looked to be a nice Tennessee buck.

The deer meandered near the place on the logging road where they usually turned right and walked by my treestand. Finally the buck was within 20 yards of the trail, and my pulse was at a level that would test even the strongest heart. But he ignored the trail that followed the ridge where I sat and walked right on by. I couldn't believe it! My disappointed heart sank. All I could do was watch him follow the wide sweep of the road that would lead him to the backside of the farm. But then I remembered something I had with me that might save the day.

I'd never used a grunt call in all my years of whitetail hunting. I purchased the one I had with me some time before that day and had practiced at home with the instructional cassette tape that came with the device, but I had not put it to the test in the woods. I knew my calling ability was questionable at best. I figured it was time to give it a try.

I searched for the small metal zipper tab on my jacket. I quietly pulled down on the zipper, slid my hand inside and felt around for the tube that hung around my neck at the end of a short lanyard. When I found it, I put my fingers around it and paused for a couple of seconds to process my thoughts.

The whitetail and I are different. Someone said about God and man that we're different not in degree, but in kind. The same is true for man and deer. Though we're each made of flesh and blood, and both of us have an instinct for survival, for the most part we are two completely different creatures not designed for vocally communicating with each other. Yet in my hand I held a potential link between my mind and his.

I felt a little anxious about proceeding. If I produced the wrong sound the buck's quick departure would be likely. The reservations I was feeling were quickly cast aside because the buck was getting away! In the few seconds I spent arguing with myself, he had walked on around the bend of the road and turned left, entered the timber, and was about to casually stroll out of sight. My window of opportunity was closing! I had nothing to lose but a bucketful of ego, so I mentally rehearsed the sound I had heard on the demo tape and put the call to my mouth.

Though he was out of range for my arrow I didn't think he was out of earshot for the sound of the call. With the open end of the

A hungry dog hunts best.
LEE TREVINO

tube pointed toward the buck I gently forced some air through the mouthpiece of the call. The best way to describe the short, guttural sound the device made was that it resembled a man's post-meal burp. It's actually not a lovely sound, at least to a nonhunter's ear. To me the grunt sounded like sweet music.

I was surprised at how much the call favored the demonstrations I had listened to on the tape. I was duly impressed with the sound I had made, but I was much more excited by what I saw immediately after the call went forth. The walking deer stopped dead in his tracks and looked my way. Though I had no idea what I had just said to him, I was hoping his interpretation of my call was, "I'm one of you. Come back here!"

As if he had thought it through and decided his ears were playing tricks on him, he started to walk away again. When he did I quickly put the call to my mouth and blew just a little bit louder. He stopped again and slightly turned his head toward me. I couldn't see his face clearly, but I imagined it had an expression that said, "That sure did sound like another deer. Nah…it couldn't be." And then he walked on again.

When he took a couple of more steps I realized one more try would probably be the last hurrah for my first attempt to communicate with a deer. I cast aside all inhibition, put the call to my lips, and gave it a rather forceful, louder, longer, and more confident burst of air. I still wasn't sure what the call would say to the buck, but what I wanted him to hear this time was, "I'm here to steal your girlfriend, Bubba!"

The call must have sounded like some sort of threat because the thrill of what happened next made me nearly fall out of my stand. He stopped and abruptly turned his head precisely in my direction and gave an aggressive-looking stare. Though I was sure he couldn't see me among the foliage, it appeared he knew exactly where the source of the sound was located. Thankfully the slight breeze was coming from him to me so I knew if he decided to check me out the conditions were in my favor.

For about three seconds that seemed like minutes he looked behind himself. Suddenly he wheeled around on his back hooves and began walking toward my stand. My legs shook with excitement as I replaced the tube in my jacket and zipped it up to make sure that if I got a shot the bowstring wouldn't catch on it.

When he crossed back over the logging road and entered the section of the woods where I was, he was on a brisk, deliberate pace. As he walked, his head went side to side like radar, obviously looking to find the challenging intruder. He didn't look downward to the ground as he came, so I knew I would have to wait for the moment his

To be sure of hitting the target, shoot first, and call whatever you hit the target.

ASHLEIGH BRILLIANT

eyes would go behind a huge oak that stood between us about 20 yards out. I instantly calculated that the angle he would walk as he went by the tree would provide about two seconds for me to get to full draw. It would be my only chance to not be detected by his very keen eyes.

When he reached the oak I put every ounce of strength I could muster into getting to full draw. My excited arm muscles trembled as I pulled back on the taut string. Finally the peep sight was at my eye, and I quickly found fur in the opening.

As the buck came closer I assumed he would walk right on by me. He suddenly came to an abrupt halt and stood broadside a mere 12 yards from my stand. Somehow his incredible sense of hearing and his amazing ability to calculate the distance from his ear drums to sound source seemed to make him aware of exactly how far to walk. While he paused, I put my 15-yard sight pin on the lower area of his vitals and slowly put pressure on the release trigger. The bow recoiled in my hands as the arrow began its short flight.

The slap of the bow limbs as they collapsed probably sounded like the blast of a gun shot in the quiet of the timber, but I didn't hear it. I also didn't hear the buck dig into the thick blanket of dried leaves as he made his explosive departure. All I knew in that instant was that the many things that must go right in order for a dream to become reality in the deer hunter's woods had done just that. Not only had I arrowed a nice Tennessee buck, it was the first time ever that I had managed to talk an animal into coming to me. The fatally wounded buck didn't run but 20 yards, staggered, and within mere seconds was transferred from nature's care to the responsibility of Grissom's Meats, my favorite local wild game processor, who would receive him later that morning.

I stood there amazed that a simple combination of a little bit of breath passing through a plastic tube over a thin reed would yield such a result. Using my extremely limited whitetail vocabulary, I had spoken a language that a creature so vastly different than me had understood, believed, and accepted. My call had spanned the huge communication gap between animal and man.

The Heart of a Passion

FISHING AND HUNTING have been longtime winners on our home's list of enjoyable things to do, at least for me and my two children, Nathan and Heidi. My wife, Annie, has never taken to the idea of sitting for hours on a deer stand or handling wiggly nightcrawlers with her bare hands. The kids and I understand her reluctance to venture too far outdoors past her flower garden, but we appreciate her willingness to embrace our adventures.

As it turned out, there was a convenient division of interests that developed among our children when it came to the water and woods. Heidi took to fishing with a passion that would rival Simon Peter and his brother Andrew. Nathan, on the other hand, was our Nimrod—a true hunter. In the middle was a papa who desperately loves to do both. I could not have taken a state-of-the-art computer and engineered a better situation for myself. To have two kids whose affections were so evenly disbursed allowed me to span the entire year in the pleasure of entertaining the joy they each found in the outdoors. What a blessing!

Of all the elements of each activity I wanted to teach them, perhaps one of the most important had to do with attitude more than aptitude. While showing them skills such as casting and shooting was a great deal of fun for me, there was something to be learned that was of greater import. I wanted them to deeply respect the life of the creatures we would capture and consume. To go to a deer stand or a lake without regard for the blood that flowed through the veins of an animal or a fish was not allowed. There had to be an understanding that while we as humans have dominion over all that flies, crawls, or swims, these creatures do have feelings.

I managed to teach Nathan and Heidi that shedding the blood of the game had to be accompanied by a certain remorse. Without it, we would merely be murderers. I realize there seems to be a great conflict between these two ideas. But believing that mankind has a right to "harvest" the fish, furry animals, and birds for food means we are not restricted from the pursuit. While we admittedly enjoy the challenge of developing and using the skills required to outsmart our prey, we cannot come to the moment of taking their lives with a casual spirit.

Many nights following a kill earlier in the day, I have laid my head on my pillow and been unable to fall quickly to sleep. I know it sounds odd, but I am invariably haunted by the sight of a creature that has died at my hands. I can only hope that my children will carry this strange irony of the heart through their hunting and fishing years.

*It has always been my private conviction
that any man who pits
his intelligence against a fish and loses
has it coming.*

JOHN STEINBECK

*Three-fourths of the Earth's surface
is water and one-fourth is land.
It is quite clear that the good Lord intended
us to spend triple the amount of time
fishing as taking care of the lawn.*
CHUCK CLARK

Grilled Fish Fillets with Cilantro Lime Butter

LINDSEY WILLIAMS

This delicious recipe works great with tuna, swordfish, wahoo, salmon, red snapper...you name it.
The cilantro lime butter will hook your friends.

Cilantro Lime Butter

3 tablespoons butter, softened
2 teaspoons freshly grated lime zest
2 tablespoons fresh lime juice
2 small fresh garlic cloves, minced
2 tablespoons minced fresh cilantro leaves

Mix in a small bowl together, and salt and pepper to taste.

Brush fillets (a meaty fish grills best) with olive oil. Lightly salt and pepper the fillets. Grill fish on an oiled rack set 5 to 6 inches above glowing coals until cooked through and firm to the touch.

Top each fillet with a dollop of cilantro lime butter and serve with rice and a fresh garden salad.

For the supreme test of a fisherman
is not how many fish he has caught,
not even how he has caught them,
but what he has caught when he has caught no fish.

JOHN H. BRADLEY

TIME TO PUT OFF THE WORLD AND GO SOMEWHERE

AND FIND MY HEALTH AGAIN IN THE SEARCH.

W.B. YEATS

*I went to the woods because I wished
to live deliberately, to front only
the essential facts of life, and see if
I could not learn what it had to teach, and not,
when I came to die, discover that I had not lived.*

HENRY DAVID THOREAU

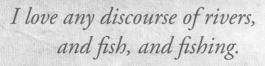

*I love any discourse of rivers,
and fish, and fishing.*
IZAAK WALTON

The most affectionate creature in the world is a wet dog.
AMBROSE BIERCE

Hunting, fishing, drawing,
and music occupied my every moment.
Cares I knew not, and cared naught about them.

JOHN JAMES AUDUBON

I CAN CONFIDENTLY SAY that as far as I'm concerned sitting alone on a deer stand has not once felt like drudgery. Even when I head home empty-handed I still feel refreshed for having been out there. And just because we hunters might go home with an unpunched tag doesn't mean we're leaving the woods skunked. There have been times when I've left the stand with the memory of a sunrise so lovely that I was reminded to say a quiet "thank You!" to the Creator. Is that a trophy? You bet!